HAL•LEONARD INSTRUMENTAL PLAY-ALONG

TROMBONE

AUDIO ACCESS INCLUDED

PLAYBACK+
Speed • Pitch • Balance • Loop

Disney MARY POP[redacted]JRNS

MUSIC BY MARC SHAIMAN
LYRICS BY SCOTT WITTMAN AND MARC SHAIMAN

Can You Imagine That?....................................2

A Conversation 4

A Cover Is Not the Book..................................5

(Underneath the) Lovely London Sky................6

Nowhere to Go But Up....................................8

The Place Where Lost Things Go 10

The Royal Doulton Music Hall 11

Trip a Little Light Fantastic 12

Turning Turtle 14

Audio Arrangements by Peter Deneff

To access audio, visit:
www.halleonard.com/mylibrary

Enter Code
3026-3431-2316-0469

ISBN 978-1-5400-4591-1

HAL•LEONARD®

Visit Hal Leonard Online at
www.halleonard.com

Contact us:
Hal Leonard
7777 West Bluemound Road
Milwaukee, WI 53213
Email: info@halleonard.com

In Europe, contact:
Hal Leonard Europe Limited
42 Wigmore Street
Marylebone, London, W1U 2RN
Email: info@halleonardeurope.com

In Australia, contact:
Hal Leonard Australia Pty. Ltd.
4 Lentara Court
Cheltenham, Victoria, 3192 Australia
Email: info@halleonard.com.au

CAN YOU IMAGINE THAT?

TROMBONE

Music by MARC SHAIMAN
Lyrics by SCOTT WITTMAN and MARC SHAIMAN

f
f
ff

A CONVERSATION

TROMBONE

Music by MARC SHAIMAN
Lyrics by SCOTT WITTMAN and MARC SHAIMAN

A COVER IS NOT THE BOOK

TROMBONE

Music by MARC SHAIMAN
Lyrics by SCOTT WITTMAN and MARC SHAIMAN

(Underneath the)
LOVELY LONDON SKY

TROMBONE

Music by MARC SHAIMAN
Lyrics by SCOTT WITTMAN and MARC SHAIMAN

rit.
p
mf a tempo
2
f
mf
rit.
f
a tempo
mf
mp
rit.
p

NOWHERE TO GO BUT UP

TROMBONE

Music by MARC SHAIMAN
Lyrics by SCOTT WITTMAN and MARC SHAIMAN

f
mp
mf
f

THE PLACE WHERE LOST THINGS GO

TROMBONE

Music by MARC SHAIMAN
Lyrics by SCOTT WITTMAN and MARC SHAIMAN

THE ROYAL DOULTON MUSIC HALL

TROMBONE

Music by MARC SHAIMAN
Lyrics by SCOTT WITTMAN and MARC SHAIMAN

TRIP A LITTLE LIGHT FANTASTIC

TROMBONE

Music by MARC SHAIMAN
Lyrics by SCOTT WITTMAN and MARC SHAIMAN

2

TURNING TURTLE

TROMBONE

Music by MARC SHAIMAN
Lyrics by SCOTT WITTMAN and MARC SHAIMAN

4
mf
1.
2.
f
Slowly
mp
Tempo I
mf
cresc. poco a poco
f
ff